W9-AHH-511

DATE DUE

BENJAMIN HARRISON

PRESIDENTIAL ✦ LEADERS

BENJAMIN HARRISON

BRUCE ADELSON

TWENTY-FIRST CENTURY BOOKS/MINNEAPOLIS

This book is dedicated to my son Michael – My special hero.

Twenty-First Century Books
A division of Lerner Publishing Group
241 First Avenue North
Minneapolis, MN 55401 U.S.A.

Website address: www.lernerbooks.com

Library of Congress Cataloging-in-Publication Data

Adelson, Bruce.
    Benjamin Harrison / by Bruce Adelson.
        p. cm. — (Presidential leaders)
    Includes bibliographical references and index.
    ISBN-13: 978–0–8225–1497–8 (lib. bdg. : alk. paper)
    ISBN-10: 0–8225–1497–4 (lib. bdg. : alk. paper)
    1. Harrison, Benjamin, 1833–1901—Juvenile literature.   2. Presidents—United States—Biography—Juvenile literature. I. Title. II. Series.
E702.A33 2007
973.8'6092—dc22   2005032100

Manufactured in the United States of America
1 2 3 4 5 6 – JR – 12 11 10 09 08 07

10-8-08

CONTENTS

❖

*Benjamin Harrison grew up in this house on his family's farm in
North Bend, Ohio.*

INTRODUCTION

BORN TO BE PRESIDENT

Time only can tell; but we do not think that Benjamin will miss his chance to write his page in the history of the United States.
—The *Columbia (SC) Record*, on the 1889 inauguration of President Benjamin Harrison

In many ways, Benjamin Harrison was a typical young boy. Growing up on a farm in the mid-1800s in Ohio, he enjoyed playing in the fields and woods with his brothers and sisters. He also enjoyed visiting his grandfather's farm, right next door. He loved visiting his grandfather's library and looking through the large collection of books on history and politics. He spent many hours sitting on the front steps of his grandfather's farmhouse, listening to his grandfather tell stories.

But in one way, Benjamin Harrison was not typical at all. Unlike most Ohio farm boys of the era, he came from a famous family. His grandfather, William Henry Harrison, had been a war hero, a governor, a member of Congress, and finally the ninth president of the United States. His great-grandfather, also named Benjamin Harrison, had signed the Declaration of Independence. Other ancestors had also been prominent statesmen and soldiers.

Unfortunately, shortly after becoming president, William Henry Harrison had died of pneumonia. The death was a sad blow for young Benjamin, who was just seven years old when his grandfather died. But the loss only increased his pride in his grandfather and the Harrison family.

A FAMILY OF PATRIOTS

The first famous Harrison was Thomas Harrison. Born in Scotland in the early 1600s, he served as a member of Parliament, the national legislature of Great Britain. He also served as a British army general in the mid-1600s. In the early 1700s, Thomas Harrison's descendants left Scotland for the American colony Virginia.

In America the Harrisons continued their tradition of public service. One of Thomas Harrison's descendants settled in the small Virginia town of Berkeley, where Benjamin Harrison V was born in 1726. Like other relatives, this Benjamin Harrison entered politics. In 1764 he was elected to Virginia's legislature, called the House of Burgesses. After assuming office, he quickly discovered how strained relations had become between America and Great Britain. Like many other Americans, he supported America's independence from Great Britain. He became a leader in the American Revolution (1775–1783), and in 1776 he signed the Declaration of Independence.

Benjamin's son William Henry wanted adventure. So in 1798, he moved with his young family to North Bend, Ohio, then part of the American frontier. From 1801 to 1812, William Henry served as the first governor of the Indiana Territory, west of Ohio. But he became better known as an army general. In 1811 his troops fought a force of Native Americans at Tippecanoe Creek in Indiana. In the War of 1812 (1812–1815), fought against Great Britain, Harrison led his troops in several battles against the British and their Native American allies.

When the war ended, General Harrison moved back to Ohio, where he resumed his political career. He became a U.S. congressmember, an Ohio state senator, a U.S. senator, and eventually, in 1841, the ninth president of the United States.

By then, William Henry Harrison had many grand-children, including young Benjamin. Named after his Revolutionary War hero great-grandfather, Benjamin Harrison knew that much was expected of him. He made up his mind early that he would serve his country, just as other Harrisons had done before him. In many ways, even as a young boy, Benjamin's path was already determined. The path would lead him to the highest office in the United States—one his grandfather had held briefly—the presidency.

CHAPTER ONE

GROWING UP OUT WEST

*[Benjamin is] determined to go
ahead in everything.*
—schoolteacher Harriet Root

In the late 1820s, the Harrisons were a well-known and wealthy Ohio family. By then William Henry Harrison was a U.S. senator. His son John Scott Harrison managed the family farm in North Bend, Ohio. John's portion of the farm, called the Point, was a gift from his father. The Point encompassed six hundred acres and produced mostly corn, wheat, and hay.

North Bend was near Cincinnati in southern Ohio, at the mouth of the Miami River and near the Ohio River. At the time, Ohio was considered part of the western United States, on the young country's frontier. To the west lay Native American territory and land largely unexplored by white people.

Benjamin's father, John Scott Harrison (left), managed the large family farm.

✧ ————————

John Harrison and his wife, Lucretia Knapp Johnson Harrison, had three children: Elizabeth, William, and Sarah. In 1829 William died when he was just two and a half years old. More tragedy struck the family the following year. After giving birth to Sarah, Lucretia became weaker and weaker. Sarah's birth had been difficult, and the doctors were uncertain if Lucretia would survive. She died in 1830, leaving her husband to manage two children and a large farm by himself.

Soon after his wife's death, John Harrison remarried, this time wedding Elizabeth Ramsey Irwin. The couple's first child, Archibald, was born in June 1832. On August 20, 1833, John and Elizabeth welcomed a second child. They named him Benjamin, after John's grandfather. Eventually, John and Elizabeth had eight more children.

Benjamin's mother, Elizabeth (left), had ten children of her own, plus two step-children.

✧ ————————————

The Harrisons were a hardworking farm family. Benjamin and the other children had lots of chores to do. Benjamin carried wood into the house for heating and cooking fires. He helped wash dishes and feed the many farm animals, including cows and horses.

Farmwork was hard for the red-headed Benjamin, who was a short boy and not physically strong. But Benjamin loved the outdoors and farm life. He much preferred North Bend, with its clean country air, to the big city of Cincinnati. For fun, Benjamin swam and fished in the Miami River and hunted small animals in the woods. He liked exploring the riverbank, walking among the reeds and bulrushes and look-ing for animals that lived on the river's edge.

A SURPRISE DISCOVERY

There, along the banks of the Miami River, one day young Benjamin encountered a young black man—a runaway slave. Slavery was illegal in Ohio and other Northern states, but slavery flourished in the Southern states.

The area around Cincinnati, with its many rivers forming a border with the South, was a popular place for slaves fleeing their Southern masters. Early nineteenth-century laws made it a crime to help runaway slaves. Nevertheless, many people in southern Ohio opposed slavery. They helped runaway slaves make their way to places such as New York, Massachusetts, and Canada, where slavery was not allowed.

The slave Benjamin met was a frightened young man. Both were too startled to speak to each other when they met. Benjamin had heard of slavery but did not know much about it. But he knew from his father and grandfather that the Harrison family had long opposed slavery.

The runaway slave did not stay on the riverbank long. As Benjamin watched, the young man quickly moved inland, to get away from his old master and other people trying to hunt him down and return him to slavery.

PRAYER AND HARD WORK

Benjamin's father and mother were deeply religious people. The family attended a local Presbyterian church every Sunday. Prayer was a regular part of their family life. John and Elizabeth were strict parents and were not affectionate with their children.

John Harrison expected a lot from his children. He especially had big plans for Benjamin. After all, the

Benjamin's great-grandfather (above) was one of the signers of the Declaration of Independence.

————————————— ◇ —————————————

Harrisons had named Benjamin for his father's grandfather, a signer of the Declaration of Independence. Benjamin often heard stories about his famous relatives and the important roles they had played in the history of the United States. His parents expected Benjamin, perhaps more than his brothers and sisters, to be the next Harrison to add to his family's reputation. His parents believed he had a special spark and intelligence.

FARM BUSINESS

John Harrison sold his farm products on the world market. He had his grain loaded onto flatboats and shipped down the Miami River to the Mississippi River, then all the way to New Orleans, Louisiana. There, oceangoing ships carried the products to Caribbean and European countries. Benjamin loved watching crews load the long flatboats with box after box of farm products. He also enjoyed talking to the crews about their adventures on the big Mississippi River, which Benjamin had never seen.

───────────────── ❖ ─────────────────

Boats traveled down the Mississippi River, carrying people and goods to New Orleans and the rest of the world.

To assure that merchants handled his cargo properly, Benjamin's father often accompanied the flatboats down the Mississippi. This work kept him away from home for long periods. But despite John Harrison's efforts, the family farm never earned a profit. John was often in debt and had to borrow money from friends and relatives to keep the farm running.

SLAVERY IN AMERICA

Slavery came to North America in the early 1600s. Slaves were captured in Africa and shipped to the American colonies. They and their descendants were forced to work on large farms called plantations, mostly in the American South. Slaves had no freedom and were the property of their owners, called masters. Slaves worked without pay in their owners' fields and houses, picking cotton, washing clothes, cleaning, and performing other household and farm tasks.

By the early 1800s, many people in the North opposed slavery and wanted it abolished, or banned, throughout the United States. Many Southerners supported slavery and disliked people from other parts of the country telling them what to do. In the early and mid-1800s, as the United States added more states and territories, people in the North and South argued about whether slavery should be allowed in these new areas. Sometimes lawmakers made compromises, permitting slavery in one new state but not another. But many Americans felt that such compromises just delayed the inevitable. Once and for all, the nation would have to decide whether to allow slavery or end it.

SCHOOL DAYS

As a young boy, Benjamin attended school in a one-room log schoolhouse that his father had built on the farm. The teacher worked for Benjamin's father. The other students were his brothers and sisters and the children of some of the Harrisons' farmworkers.

Benjamin quickly impressed his first teacher, Harriet Root. Root, who had also taught the older Harrison children, later called Benjamin "the brightest of the family." She also described him as "terribly stubborn about many things." Benjamin undoubtedly inherited this trait from his father, who was also known to be stubborn and impatient.

In 1847 fourteen-year-old Benjamin and his older brother Archibald moved to Cincinnati to attend an all-boys

─────────────── ✧ ───────────────

Cincinnati was a busy city in the mid-1800s. In this illustration, horses and carriages travel along a street by the river.

prep school called Farmers College. This private school was designed to give young men a thorough education to prepare them for work or university studies. At Farmers, Benjamin especially enjoyed studying history, politics, and sociology. He wrote papers about the American Revolution, the War of 1812, and other events in American history.

Benjamin's favorite teacher was Robert Bishop, who had served as president of Miami University before working at Farmers. Under Bishop's supervision, Benjamin became an excellent student. He was interested in learning and curious about the world. He became friendly with Caroline Scott, the daughter of the Reverend John Scott, a chemistry and physics professor at Farmers. Caroline, one year older than Benjamin, attracted him with her beauty and lively personality.

HIGHER EDUCATION

John Harrison had big dreams for his son. He wanted Benjamin to attend a famous eastern university, such as Harvard or Yale, and then become a minister. John thought that an education at a top-name school would help Benjamin in his future career. But John Harrison's debts continued. When it was time for Benjamin to go to a university, John could not afford to send his son to an expensive eastern school.

Instead, Benjamin enrolled at nearby Miami University. Benjamin had first learned about the all-male university from his teacher Robert Bishop. The school was in Oxford, Ohio, about twenty-five miles north of Cincinnati and North Bend. Benjamin's academic success at Farmers

College qualified him to skip his first two years of university studies and enter Miami as a junior.

In August 1850, the summer before Benjamin was scheduled to start college, his mother gave birth to a son, James. The birth was difficult, and it seriously weakened Elizabeth Harrison. She never recovered and died just days before Benjamin left for school. (Shortly afterward, the baby also died.) Although terribly saddened by his mother's death, Benjamin began college on time.

Harrison became a lawyer after finishing his studies at Miami University.

CHAPTER TWO

THE YOUNG LAWYER

*It is quite . . . illogical to despise a man because
he is rich as because he is poor. Not what a
man has, but what he is, settles his class.*
—Benjamin Harrison

Benjamin Harrison began his studies at Miami University
in September 1850. He was known as a smart, stern, quiet,
and religious student. He joined the local Presbyterian
church and regularly attended services there. Outside the
classroom, Harrison did not spend much time with his
fellow students.

In the classroom, Harrison quickly discovered that he
had a gift for public speaking. He impressed his classmates with the power of his words and his ability to think
quickly. He joined the Union Literary Society, a college
club, and became its president. Society members read and
discussed books and debated many subjects, such as liter-
ature, world and American history, and politics.

Sometimes Harrison gave speeches on these subjects to his teachers and classmates.

Harrison's idol was Patrick Henry, a hero of the American Revolution and one of the great public speakers of the revolutionary period. Henry had been a confident and forceful public figure. His speeches were meant to inspire his listeners and convince them of his points of view. Harrison tried to pattern his speaking style after Patrick Henry's. Like Henry, Harrison wanted his audiences to follow his words and agree with what he was telling them.

✧ ———————————
Patrick Henry, a leader of the Revolutionary War era, was famous for saying, "Give me liberty, or give me death."

Although John Harrison wanted his son to become a Presbyterian minister, Harrison decided that he'd rather be a lawyer. His skill at public speaking and his ease in discussing many different subjects most likely influenced his decision.

Although not the friendliest person on the Miami campus, Harrison became a different man around Caroline Scott, his old friend from his days at Farmers College. Caroline had become a student at Oxford Female Institute, Miami's "sister school," where all the students were women. Caroline Scott's father, Reverend John Scott, had moved to Oxford with his family to head the Oxford Female Institute.

———————————— ✧ ————————————

Reverend John Scott was the father of Caroline Scott.
This photograph of him was taken in 1888.

Caroline and Harrison began seeing each other often. She was everything he was not. Although she was an attractive woman, her social skills were her true strength. She was outgoing, friendly, and spirited, and she loved to dance. Harrison hated dancing. What's more, his religion forbade it. Nevertheless, Caroline often brought Benjamin to dances with her. Short, with red hair and a red beard, Harrison was not easily missed at these dances. He stood against the wall, usually talking to no one, waiting for Caroline to finish dancing.

Harrison and Caroline soon fell in love. He sent her many affectionate, moving letters, showing a warm side of his personality that few people ever saw. Harrison called his new girlfriend Carrie. The couple became engaged, but they decided to delay their marriage until Benjamin had become a lawyer and Carrie had graduated from college.

In 1852 Harrison graduated from Miami University. He ranked fourth in his class of about 250 students and received high academic honors. At the graduation ceremony, he gave a speech titled, "The Poor of England," about the causes of poverty among British citizens. His audience was impressed.

NEW BEGINNINGS

Most people interested in legal careers in this era did not go to law school. Instead, they learned their profession by working as apprentices (lawyers-in-training) to established lawyers. Harrison became an apprentice with the Storer and Gwynne law firm of Cincinnati. He worked at the firm for about two years and gained a thorough legal education. Carrie, meanwhile, stayed in Oxford. She lived with her parents while finishing her last year of college. After her graduation, she worked in Oxford as a music teacher.

On October 20, 1853, Benjamin Harrison married Caroline Lavinia Scott. He was twenty, and she was twenty-one. The wedding took place in Oxford, and the bride's father performed the ceremony. At Caroline's request, few guests attended the wedding, and the ceremony was simple. The newlyweds spent their honeymoon at North Bend, on the Harrison family farm.

Life was also changing for Benjamin Harrison's father, John. Late in 1853, the U.S. congressional representative from the North Bend area left office, creating an unexpected vacancy. John Harrison was busy with his farm, but local political leaders urged him to run for the congressional seat. They believed that the son of President William Henry Harrison would be a popular candidate. They were right. John Harrison ran for Congress in 1853 as a member of the Whig Party, the political party of his father, and won the election.

MAKING A NAME FOR HIMSELF

In 1854 Benjamin Harrison was admitted to the bar, a professional association of lawyers. He was authorized to practice law on his own. The Harrisons decided to move to Indianapolis, Indiana, where Harrison would begin his legal career.

By then, Carrie was pregnant. Shortly after the couple moved to Indianapolis, she returned to Oxford to have the baby with the help of her family. The child, Russell Benjamin Harrison, was born on August 12, 1854. Harrison remained in Indianapolis alone until Carrie and the baby were well enough to return to Indianapolis. The new family moved into a small home on East Vermont Street.

Harrison quickly earned a reputation as an excellent attorney, thorough and thoughtful in his work. In the courtroom, he impressed judges and other lawyers with his legal arguments. In addition to his private practice, he worked part-time arguing cases on behalf of the city of Indianapolis. In his first case, he prosecuted (carried out legal proceedings against) a man charged with burglary. The man was found guilty and sent to jail.

As his reputation grew, several other attorneys asked Harrison to form partnerships with them. Harrison selected an accomplished lawyer named William Wallace as his partner. Together, they developed a very successful law practice.

NEW GOALS

As Harrison became more prominent in Indianapolis, he began thinking about another career, one that would build on his growing good reputation. He considered following in the footsteps of his father, grandfather, and great-grandfather by entering politics.

His father belonged to the Whig Party, as had his grandfather. But that party was growing weaker in the United States. So in 1856, Harrison joined the new Republican Party. He thought this brand-new political party offered many opportunities for a young lawyer with a famous name. He also favored the antislavery position held by many in the Republican Party.

That year Harrison campaigned for John Frémont, the Republicans' first candidate for president of the United

Harrison supported John Frémont (right) in the 1856 presidential campaign.

States. Frémont lost the election, but the Republican Party kept growing. John Harrison, who had expected his son to join the Whig Party like his ancestors, was disappointed by his son's involvement with the Republicans.

In 1857 Benjamin Harrison decided to enter politics himself. Running as the Republican candidate, he won the office of Indianapolis city attorney. He was in charge of providing legal advice and representation to the city. The job paid only four hundred dollars a year (a meager salary in 1857), but Harrison considered the position a good first step toward a political career. He set aside his private practice to take the job.

On April 3, 1858, the Harrisons had their second child, Mary Scott Harrison. With two young children, their modest home seemed even smaller. Money was sometimes tight, and the family had to limit their spending on food and other household items. Harrison felt pressure to earn more money. Normally gruff with business colleagues, he treated his children with great affection. Carrie, as was typical for the time, was a full-time mother who did not work outside the Harrison home.

Indiana Republican Party leaders considered Harrison, with his famous name, thriving law practice, and successful first run for political office, a rising star. They picked him to be the state party's secretary. In this position, which he held in addition to practicing law, he kept track

of Republican Party members across Indiana. He also traveled throughout the state to various party meetings. Party secretary was an important position that helped Harrison become well known throughout the

✧ ———————————

Harrison continued to build his reputation within the Republican Party by campaigning for Abraham Lincoln (left) in 1860.

state. In 1860 he campaigned for the Republicans' second presidential candidate, Abraham Lincoln. This time the Republicans were successful—Lincoln won the election.

Also in 1860, Harrison won election to his first statewide political office—supreme court reporter. As the reporter, he was responsible for summarizing all the Indiana Supreme Court's opinions, putting them in books, and then selling the books, mainly to other lawyers. With this part-time job, Harrison could continue his law practice and also keep part of the proceeds from the book sales. Harrison profited handsomely from these sales.

A YOUNG NATION TORN APART

In 1860, just when Benjamin Harrison began enjoying some financial success, the United States faced a crisis. The country was divided—North against South, neighbor against neighbor—over the issue of slavery. During the 1860 presidential race, many Southerners opposed Abraham Lincoln because he did not support slavery. Even before the election, Southerners began talking about seceding, or leaving the United States, and starting their own country—one that would allow slavery.

Shortly after Lincoln's election, the citizens of South Carolina voted to secede from the United States. More Southern states soon joined South Carolina. On February 8, 1861, representatives from seven Southern states created their own nation, named the Confederate States of America. By the end of 1861, four more Southern states had joined the Confederacy.

President Lincoln would not permit the Southern states to leave the Union (United States). He was determined to

*The Civil War started when Southern troops fired on
Fort Sumter in South Carolina.*

save the country, by force if necessary. People on both sides
prepared for war. Thousands of men joined the armies of
the Union (the North) and the Confederacy (the South).
On April 12, 1861, Confederate soldiers fired on Fort
Sumter, a U.S. fort in the harbor of Charleston, South
Carolina. The Civil War (1861–1865) had begun.

CHAPTER THREE

THE WAR WITH NO END

*Let us calmly put our trust in God
and wait the [war's end].*

—Benjamin Harrison

By 1862 the Civil War had already gone longer than anyone had thought it would. Thousands of soldiers on both sides had been killed. Thousands more had been wounded. Farms, trees, and houses had been destroyed in battles fought around them.

The war was not going well for the Union. Its army had lost many battles and many soldiers. The Confederacy remained a separate country, where slavery still existed. On July 1, 1862, President Lincoln asked for three hundred thousand more men to volunteer as soldiers for the Union army. (Later, Lincoln enacted a draft, a system that required some men to join the army.)

CALL FOR HELP

In Indiana and other states in the North, people were dissatisfied with how the war was being fought. The Union army had lost almost every large battle against the Confederates. Northerners worried about how much longer the war would last. They also were unhappy about the president's request for volunteers. Some people began to wonder if the war was even worth fighting. They thought it might be better just to let the South leave the United States. At least then, people thought, their soldiers would no longer die on the battlefield.

At first, few Indiana men listened to President Lincoln's call to volunteer for the army. Indiana governor, Oliver Perry Morton, a strong supporter of the president and the Union cause, grew worried. He knew the war was going badly for the United States and that many more soldiers would be needed to defeat the Confederates and save the Union.

Morton turned to Benjamin Harrison and William Wallace, Harrison's law partner, for their assistance in bringing Indiana men into the army. Harrison and Wallace were well known in Indiana. Governor Morton wanted to use their excellent reputations to convince people to support the Union. If Wallace and Harrison favored the war, the governor hoped other men would follow their lead and volunteer to fight the Confederates.

Harrison, also concerned that support for the war in Indiana seemed to be fading, agreed to help. Morton made Harrison an officer, with the rank of second lieutenant. He told Harrison to create a new military unit called the Seventieth Indiana Volunteer Regiment.

Benjamin Harrison bought a military cap, a fife and drum (instruments used for military music), and a U.S. flag. He hung the flag in the window of his law office. Then Harrison prepared for his new job. He told Carrie what the governor had asked him to do and started asking men to join his regiment.

Once again, Benjamin Harrison faced high expectations. Many people compared him to his grandfather, William Henry Harrison, who had won many battles fighting Native Americans in Indiana. Harrison had never liked being compared to his grandfather. "I want it understood that I am the grandson of nobody. I believe that every man

✧ ————————————
Harrison joined the war effort with the rank of second lieutenant.

should stand on his own merits," he once said. He ignored the comparisons and went about doing his job: forming a regiment of Indiana soldiers, training them to fight, and helping win the war.

COLONEL HARRISON

Harrison used the public speaking skills he had developed in college to convince his fellow Indianans that fighting for the Union was important. He made several speeches in Indiana, urging men to follow his lead, join the army, and support the United States. Within a month, about one thousand soldiers had joined his regiment. Harrison did such a good job attracting volunteer soldiers that Governor Morton promoted him to the rank of colonel and made him the regiment's commander.

As the soldiers left Indiana for war, they marched through the streets of Indianapolis. People cheered the new soldiers and wished them good luck. They traveled by railroad to Louisville, Kentucky, to begin their training. Kentucky was a Confederate state, but Union troops had secured the area around Louisville.

In Kentucky, Benjamin Harrison missed his wife and family. He wrote Carrie many letters while he was away from home. In one letter, he told her that he did not enjoy being a soldier. "I am not a Julius Caesar or Napoleon [famous generals]," he wrote. "[Instead, I am] but a plain Hoosier [Indiana] colonel, with no more relish for a fight than for a good breakfast."

Harrison was a tough teacher to his soldiers. He made strict rules, which he expected his men to follow. Many soldiers did not like Harrison. They thought he was too harsh.

What's a Hoosier?

Hoosier is a nickname for people who live in Indiana. The first use of this nickname dates to 1826. The word itself is thought to come from northwestern England, where people referred to anything very large as a hoozer. No one is sure how *hoozer* was changed to *Hoosier* and became connected to Indiana.

They also found him to be cold and unfriendly. But he was a good commanding officer who took his job seriously. After his soldiers had gone to sleep, Harrison often stayed awake, reading books about military tactics and leadership.

Eventually, the men of the Seventieth Indiana Volunteer Regiment became good soldiers. They were ready to fight Confederate troops in battle. They also came to respect their commanding officer. They affectionately nicknamed him Little Ben, because of his small size.

COMBAT WITH THE CONFEDERATES

By early 1864, the regiment had not seen much fighting. This situation changed during the spring of that year, however. Harrison's regiment was part of a larger army, commanded by General William Tecumseh Sherman. Sherman's army marched from Chattanooga, Tennessee, to Atlanta, Georgia.

Sherman's plan was to capture Atlanta, the largest and most important city in the South. Atlanta was the home of several railroad lines. The Confederate army used them to carry soldiers and supplies. Capturing Atlanta

General William Tecumseh Sherman commanded Union troops during the 1864 Civil War Battle of Atlanta.

✧ ————————————

and its railroads, Sherman knew, would damage the Confederates' ability to fight. Sherman also thought that Atlanta's capture would hurt the South's morale, since its biggest city would be in Union hands.

Marching through Tennessee and northern Georgia, Harrison's Indiana soldiers were ready for a fight. On May 13, 1864, as Harrison prepared for battle the next day, he wrote Carrie a letter. As his words show, his family was never far from his thoughts:

> *I am thinking much of you and the dear children and my whole heart comes out to you in tenderness and love....I must make this letter short, as we need a good rest tonight and shall probably be awakened early in the morning....I love you, my dear wife, with all the devotion of a full heart, and my children as the apple of my eyes.*

On July 20, Harrison and his men faced their first big challenge on the battlefield. Near Peach Tree Creek, Georgia, they met charging Confederate soldiers. As the Confederates rushed toward them, screaming at the top of their lungs, Harrison's men stood their ground and did not back down. They fought hard and forced the Confederates to retreat.

After the battle, Harrison's commanding officer was so impressed that he told the Indiana colonel, "By God Harrison. I'll make you a brigadier general for this fight." Later, Harrison and his men fought bravely at the Battle of Resaca, also in Georgia. They charged up a hill while

Confederate troops fire down on Harrison's men as they advance up a hill in the 1864 Battle of Resaca, Georgia.

Confederates fired down on them. They captured the hill and then held it when attacked.

Like his grandfather, Harrison had become a war hero. He had fought well and helped the Union win the Battle of Atlanta—as the series of battles around the city were called. On September 2, 1864, Harrison wrote to Carrie that "Atlanta is ours." The city surrendered to Union soldiers.

———————————— ✧ ————————————

After Union troops captured the city of Atlanta, they took control of the Confederate fort there.

Harrison was one of the first Union soldiers to march into the captured Confederate city.

ONCE A HOOSIER, ALWAYS A HOOSIER

On September 12, Harrison received orders to return to Indiana. Believing he was being sent home to recruit more volunteers for the army, Harrison rushed back to Indianapolis. But there were other reasons for his return. Governor Morton, also a member of the Republican Party, wanted the new Indiana war hero to help his campaign for reelection. In addition, the Indiana Republican Party had again nominated Harrison for supreme court reporter.

Morton and Harrison campaigned together, speaking to crowds of people who cheered at the sight of Colonel Harrison. At the time, only white men were allowed to vote, so Morton and Harrison addressed their words to this audience. They said that voting for them meant a vote for the soldiers fighting the Confederates. Morton and Harrison were very popular with the people of Indiana, who were excited that the Union was at last winning the war.

On October 11—Election Day in Indiana—Morton and Harrison won easily. In the national election held one month later, Abraham Lincoln also won reelection as president of the United States. Harrison spent a successful Election Day at home, celebrating the Republican Party's victories. But the Civil War hero did not stay in Indianapolis long. The war was not over. In late 1864, Harrison was ordered to return to the fighting.

In December he saw action in the Battle of Nashville in Tennessee. During the fighting, Harrison showed that he was not the cold, distant person many thought him to be.

CIVIL WAR SOLDIERS

Soldiers fighting for the Union and Confederacy used similar equipment. They carried rifles that fired a single shot at a time. After firing, the rifles had to be reloaded. To load his rifle, a soldier pushed gunpowder and a round metal bullet down the barrel. Then the soldier would prepare to fire, often while the enemy was already shooting at him.

Soldiers typically marched into battle in long lines called formations. These lines of thousands of men, marching forward with flags flying and drums and bugles playing, were easy targets for soldiers on the other side.

A group of the New York State Militia posed for this photograph in 1861.

One night, when temperatures fell below freezing, Harrison prepared a gift for his men on guard duty. Private Richard Smock wrote that he saw Colonel Harrison walking toward him with something in his hands:

> *He had a large can filled with hot coffee, and when I asked him what he was doing, he said he was afraid some of the pickets [guards] would freeze to death and he knew some hot coffee would help the men keep alive. . . . His act was one of kindness.*

Another soldier who witnessed the scene remarked: "Call such a man cold? You might as well call a volcano cold. . . . Truly, there is much God-warmth in Ben Harrison's heart."

The war ended in 1865 with the Union army victorious. During the war, President Lincoln had abolished slavery and given African Americans their freedom. More than six hundred thousand soldiers were casualties (soldiers who are killed, wounded, or captured) in this war. Soon the United States would begin to come together as one country again.

Harrison's fame as a soldier gave a boost to his politial career after the Civil War.

CHAPTER FOUR

BENJAMIN HARRISON— POLITICIAN

I have no doubt from intimations [hints] that I could go to Congress for our District at the next election, but positively I would not accept the office, for the reason that it would take me away from home so much.

—Benjamin Harrison

With the Civil War over, Harrison came home to Indiana to stay. For his bravery in the Battle of Atlanta, he was promoted to the rank of brigadier general. Then he retired from the army.

His military service had given him great confidence. He believed he had finally satisfied everyone's expectations, even his father's. At the end of the war, John Scott Harrison wrote to his son saying how proud he was of him. This was the first time Benjamin Harrison had ever received such praise from his demanding father.

Only thirty-two years old, Harrison seemed on the verge of a significant political career. He resumed his law practice and his post as supreme court reporter. His Civil War reputation helped him gain much attention and legal business. He soon represented clients in almost every important case before the Indiana courts. The Harrison family grew prosperous.

In 1867 the Harrisons moved into a new, larger house on Delaware Street in a wealthy Indianapolis neighborhood.

Harrison and his family moved into this house on Delaware Street in Indianapolis, Indiana, in 1867.

EX PARTE MILLIGAN

During the Civil War, Lambdin Milligan of Huntington, Indiana, opposed President Lincoln's drafting of men into the Union army. In 1863 Milligan gave a speech in Fort Wayne, Indiana. He argued that men should resist the draft. Soldiers arrested Milligan. He was imprisoned and charged with being a traitor to the United States. In 1864 a military court sentenced him to death.

But the U.S. Supreme Court, in the famous 1866 case of *Ex parte Milligan*, reversed the death sentence. The Court ruled that the army had had no right to arrest and try a civilian (non-military citizen). After the Supreme Court decision, Milligan sued the U.S. government, seeking money as compensation (payback) for his arrest and wrongful imprisonment.

At the request of President Ulysses S. Grant, Benjamin Harrison became the government's lawyer. He represented all

the army officers and soldiers involved in Milligan's arrest and military trial. Harrison did a brilliant job with the case. He convinced the Court that the soldiers had acted honestly. The Court ruled that the government owed Milligan compensation—but only the tiny sum of five dollars. The case made Harrison even more famous.

✦ ───────────

President Grant (left) asked Harrison to be the lawyer for the U.S. government in the 1866 case of Ex parte Milligan.

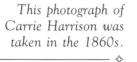

This photograph of Carrie Harrison was taken in the 1860s.

———————— ✧

The three-story brick house had sixteen rooms, a small front yard, and plenty of play space for the children. One of Harrison's favorite rooms was the library, where he spent much time reading, writing, and meeting with friends and political supporters. The house was modestly furnished, because neither Benjamin nor Carrie Harrison believed in showing off wealth or possessions.

In 1868 the Indiana Republican Party wanted Harrison to run for a seat in the U.S. House of Representatives or for Indiana governor. Harrison declined both opportunities. Instead, he wanted to spend time with his family, gain an even larger reputation in state politics, and plan for the future. He was unsure what office he would run for eventually, but he decided to bide his time. Everything seemed in place for Benjamin Harrison to become a prominent figure in U.S. politics.

POLITICAL LESSONS

In 1872 Benjamin Harrison made his first step into big-time politics. He finally wanted to run for Indiana governor, to follow Oliver Morton. He hoped that party leaders

would nominate him. But Governor Morton had become jealous of Harrison. Morton worried that his old friend was becoming too powerful. He did not want Harrison gaining even more prominence as governor. Morton made it known to his friends and colleagues that they should not support

◇ ————————

Indiana governor Morton (left) became jealous of Harrison's power and prevented his nomination for the governorship.

Harrison. Morton had much influence in Indiana, and few people wanted to anger the state's powerful governor. As a result of Morton's efforts, Harrison lost the nomination fight to a man named Thomas Browne.

This experience taught Harrison a lesson—he needed to learn more about politics and the influential people who helped candidates win elections. Despite his loss, Harrison continued to be active in politics. He campaigned enthusiastically for Ulysses S. Grant, who won reelection as president of the United States in 1872.

By 1876 Harrison had decided not to seek another term as supreme court reporter. But he continued to build his law practice and learn about politics. He refused supporters' calls for him to run for governor in 1876. He also rejected the efforts of Ohio and Indiana supporters to select him as the 1876 Republican nominee for president.

SURPRISE NOMINATION

In August, as the 1876 elections approached, Harrison took his family on a vacation to the North Shore of Lake Superior in Minnesota. The family traveled by train, the most common form of transportation in those days. By then the two Harrison children were young adults. Russell was twenty-two, and Mary was eighteen.

When he returned home from the vacation, Harrison was shocked to be greeted by cheering crowds at the Indianapolis railroad station. He learned that the Republican Party, without consulting him, had nominated him as its candidate for governor. The original Republican candidate, Godlove Orth, was accused of financial wrong-doing and had withdrawn from the race.

Surprised but honored by the nomination, Harrison accepted his party's call. Although he had refused the nomination earlier, he was a man of duty and responsibility. He felt obligated to run because his party needed him. Harrison also viewed the race as an unexpected opportunity to jump-start his political career.

Harrison did not have much time to campaign, because Orth had withdrawn only three months before the election. But Harrison worked hard and impressed party leaders with his efforts. They were also pleased with his enthusiastic campaign for Rutherford B. Hayes, the Republican candidate for president. Harrison traveled throughout the eastern and midwestern states, telling crowds that Hayes would be an excellent president.

——————————— ✧
Harrison campaigned for
Rutherford B. Hayes (right) *in*
the 1876 presidential campaign.

SHIFTING ECONOMIES

Before the Civil War, the United States had been mostly rural. Most people lived and worked on farms, far from big cities. But industrialization—the economic shift from agriculture to industry—increased during the war. Factories produced materials needed for fighting, such as guns, bullets, trains, and warships. When peace returned, the United States did not need as many weapons and other tools of war. So factory owners began manufacturing other products to keep their businesses running. They made products for the home, such as soap and furniture. Some returning soldiers and other rural dwellers moved to cities and took factory jobs. People from other nations also immigrated to U.S. cities after the war, adding to the growth of industry and urban life.

Women, as well as men, worked in factories during the period of industrialization after the Civil War.

Hayes won the election but Harrison did not. He lost the race by about five thousand votes. His late entry into the race, giving him little time to campaign across the state, most likely caused his defeat.

Despite the defeat, Republican leaders again took notice of the Civil War hero. They appreciated his vigorous, almost nonstop campaigning and his willingness to run for governor on short notice. In 1879 President Hayes rewarded Harrison for his loyalty by appointing him to the Mississippi River Commission. This federal commission supervised boat traffic and tolls, or fees charged to boats, on the Mississippi River. The commission did not meet regularly, so Harrison's job was part-time. He kept his law practice, and his family remained in Indianapolis.

NATIONAL PROMINENCE

By 1880 Benjamin Harrison appeared to be an upcoming star in U.S. politics. He led the Indiana delegation to the Republican National Convention that year. This convention, with delegates (representatives) from every state and territory, would pick the party's nominee for president. Rutherford B. Hayes had decided not to seek reelection.

The national party was split into two main groups. One wanted to nominate former president Ulysses S. Grant. The other supported U.S. senator James Blaine of Maine. Blaine was a powerful senator, with a long record of experience in foreign affairs. A few other candidates, including Treasury secretary John Sherman, were also in the running.

But the convention could not pick a nominee. The Grant and the Blaine camps were deadlocked. Ballot after ballot, delegates voted but no candidate won a majority.

Finally, after more than thirty ballots and many hours of debate, Senator Blaine withdrew his name from the race and supported another candidate, U.S. congressional representative James Garfield.

As leader of the Indiana delegation, Benjamin Harrison had to decide which candidate his state would endorse. On the thirty-fifth ballot, Harrison delivered his state's vote to Garfield. This support gave Garfield the votes necessary to become the party nominee. In November Garfield won the election and became president of the United States.

Grateful for Harrison's support, Garfield offered Harrison a cabinet post. As the president's closest advisers, cabinet members run various government agencies, such as the State Department and the Justice Department. They also advise the president on many policy matters. But Harrison declined Garfield's offer. Instead, he decided to spend more time in Indiana to strengthen his influence there.

In 1881 Harrison's hard work in his home state paid off. The state legislature elected him to the U.S. Senate. (State legislatures, not individual voters, elected senators then.)

SENATOR HARRISON

Benjamin and Carrie Harrison packed up and moved to Washington, D.C., the nation's capital. Their grown children did not move with them but stayed behind in Indiana. The Harrisons also kept their house in Indianapolis. They often returned home when Senate business permitted Harrison to leave Washington.

As a senator, Harrison supported many different policies. Most were also endorsed by the Republican Party. He successfully pushed for Civil War veterans' pensions—payments to help support former soldiers. He supported westward expansion of the United States, pushing for the admission of several new western states. He also supported the creation of a large, modern navy and the conservation of western wilderness areas, especially land along the Colorado River.

Harrison and the Republicans favored high tariffs, or taxes placed on imported products. Such tariffs were supposed to make imported goods more expensive than products made in the United States. This system made U.S. goods more appealing to consumers and helped U.S. businesses. Congress passed some high tariffs during Harrison's Senate term.

One law that Harrison opposed was the 1882 Chinese Exclusion Act. This law, supported strongly by other Republicans, was intended to keep Chinese immigrants out of the United States. Harrison did not believe in discriminating against Chinese immigrants. In addition, he believed the bill violated an agreement between the United States and China.

—————————————— ✧ ——————————————

In the late 1800s, many Chinese immigrants made their way to the west coast of the United States in crowded steamships.

CHINESE IMMIGRATION

In the late 1800s, thousands of Chinese immigrants moved to the United States, mostly to California and other western regions. Many of these immigrants found jobs in mines and on railroads. Some Americans worried that Chinese immigrants were willing to work for less money than other workers. This willingness, some Americans feared, would convince employers to hire Chinese immigrants instead of U.S.-born citizens.

Claiming that it was necessary to protect their jobs, many Americans backed the Chinese Exclusion Act of 1882. The act barred most Chinese immigration and prohibited Chinese people already living in the United States from becoming U.S. citizens. Congress passed the bill, but President Chester Arthur, who took office after James Garfield was assassinated, vetoed (refused to sign) it, saying that it violated treaties with China. Benjamin Harrison, then a senator, also opposed the law. Congress then proposed a new version of the Chinese Exclusion Act. It prohibited Chinese immigration into the United States for ten years. President Arthur signed this bill, making it law.

———————— ✧

In the 1800s, Chinese laborers helped build the Union Pacific Railroad. Many Chinese railroad workers did backbreaking labor and dangerous work with explosives.

He refused to support the act, although a version of it eventually passed Congress and became law.

When it was time for the 1884 presidential election, many Harrison supporters again wanted him to seek the party's nomination. As before, Harrison resisted, believing his time had not yet arrived. He was a patient man. He would run for office only when he thought he had the best chance to win. Instead, he enthusiastically supported the candidacy of Republican James Blaine, who lost to Democrat Grover Cleveland in a close contest.

Also in 1884, both Harrison children were married. Russell Harrison, by then working as an engineer, married Mary Saunders in Omaha, Nebraska. Mary Harrison married James McKee and settled down in Indianapolis.

Harrison's grandson, Benjamin Harrison McKee,
was known as Baby McKee.

CHAPTER FIVE

HARRISON MAKES HIS MOVE

*[Benjamin Harrison] is a very true and
very sincere man. He gains in my regard
I may say daily.*

—James Blaine, Republican opponent

By 1887 Benjamin Harrison had become one of the Republican Party's most prominent members. But he lost his bid for reelection to the U.S. Senate that year because Democrats had taken over the Indiana legislature. They refused to elect a Republican senator. The year had a bright spot, however. The Harrisons' daughter, Mary, gave birth to a son, whom she named Benjamin Harrison McKee.

The next year, Harrison finally set his sights on the ultimate political prize—the presidency. He and Carrie moved home to Indiana to prepare for the coming campaign. But Harrison didn't announce his candidacy right away. He knew that James Blaine, the Republican's leading candidate for the nomination, would be a powerful opponent. Not wanting to oppose Blaine immediately and risk a premature defeat, Harrison decided not to campaign for the nomination before the Republican National Convention. The Democrats were already set to nominate Grover Cleveland, the incumbent (sitting) president.

CAMPAIGN STRATEGY

At the time, the United States was a politically polarized (divided) country. It was split almost evenly between Democrats and Republicans. After the Civil War, the South had become solidly Democratic. So President Cleveland could count on winning every Southern state in the election. The Republicans' strongest support was in New England and the Midwest. Very few states—only Indiana, New York, Connecticut, and New Jersey—were considered swing states (states that could be won by either the Democratic or Republican candidate).

✧ ————————————

As a Democrat, President Cleveland could count on the votes of the Southern states in the 1888 election.

Of these states, Indiana and New York had the most people and therefore had the most weight in the presidential election. The Republicans considered this situation as they tried to choose the strongest possible candidate for the campaign.

Several weeks before the Republican convention, James Blaine withdrew from the nomination race. He believed that after his loss to Grover Cleveland in 1884, he might have a difficult time winning the nomination again. Instead of creating a tough nomination fight, which could threaten the party's chances against Cleveland, Blaine wanted to unite the party behind one man. He expressed confidence in two candidates: Ohio senator and former Treasury secretary John Sherman, and Benjamin Harrison. But most people suspected that Blaine was leaning toward Harrison. Four months earlier, Blaine had said that "[t]he one man remaining who . . . can make the best run is Benjamin Harrison."

As the convention neared, Harrison finally announced his candidacy. More than twelve other candidates, including John Sherman, were running. At the convention in Chicago, delegates from every state and territory gathered to cast their votes. The areas with the largest populations had the most votes at the convention.

After the first round of balloting, John Sherman had the most votes, but he did not have the majority needed to win the nomination. Harrison placed fifth. After three more rounds, Sherman remained the leader, but he still did not have a big enough majority. With each round, Sherman collected fewer and fewer votes, until finally he dropped out, believing that he could not win the nomination.

The Gilded Age

After the Civil War, the United States grew and changed as never before. Big businesses started appearing across the nation. Factories produced record amounts of iron and steel. Gold and silver were mined in large quantities. Vast forests were cut for lumber, and railroad lines expanded. All this activity created much wealth for business owners. In fact, the period from 1880 through the early 1900s is known as the Gilded (gold-covered) Age for the incredible wealth enjoyed by some Americans. Men such as John D. Rockefeller (in the oil industry) and Andrew Carnegie (in the steel industry) created huge businesses during this era.

But while a few people were very rich during the Gilded Age,

✧ ——————————

Andrew Carnegie was one of the wealthiest Americans during the Gilded Age.

While the owners of large industries were very rich, the people who made up the workforce, such as these miners, were often very poor.

most Americans were not. In 1890 more than 90 percent of U.S. households earned only $1,200 per year—barely enough for survival. In factories, mines, and other workplaces, most laborers had little power. Wages were low, and working conditions were harsh and unsafe. Labor unions, associations formed to fight for workers' rights, were small and not very powerful in the late 1800s.

After the fourth ballot, Chauncey Depew, a wealthy New Yorker who owned railroads, withdrew from the contest. He decided that he also could not win enough votes to capture the nomination. Without a New Yorker running for the nomination, the large New York delegation, with seventy-two votes, looked for someone else to support.

By then, Harrison was perfectly positioned. All other big-name candidates had dropped out, leaving Harrison as the one candidate everyone could agree upon. Many Republicans thought that his being from Indiana, an important swing state, could help the party win that state in the election. The New York delegation decided to vote for Harrison.

✧ —————————————

This flyer for the 1888 Republican Convention features two former Republican presidents: Abraham Lincoln (center) and James Garfield (right). On the far left, Theodore Roosevelt, a young Republican, waves a flag.

James Blaine supported the nomination of Harrison as the 1888 Republican presidential candidate.

❖ ——————————

With the added support of James Blaine, who sent word from Scotland about his preference, Harrison's nomination bid looked very strong. By the eighth ballot, Little Ben from Indiana—grandson of a president, son of a congressional representative—had won. He was the Republican nominee for president.

To Benjamin Harrison, this was a satisfying moment. He had waited a long time, patiently supporting the party while other Republicans moved ahead of him. Finally, Harrison was at the top of his party.

HARRISON FOR PRESIDENT

The Republicans quickly got behind their nominee. In the late 1800s, political parties were very powerful. Party leaders controlled the appointment of public officials and sometimes even bribed officeholders to get jobs and business deals. In many states, one very powerful leader controlled

Thomas Platt was a powerful leader in the Republican Party in the late 1800s and early 1900s.

✧ ——————————

the whole state party. In New York, Thomas "Boss" Platt ran the Republican Party. In Pennsylvania, Matthew Quay was the boss. These two men decided to work hard for Harrison's election. Quay became Harrison's campaign manager. They expected to be rewarded with their own government jobs, jobs for their supporters, or money if Harrison won.

President Cleveland believed that the president should be above campaigning and not ask the public for its votes. Therefore, he did not campaign at all during the election of 1888. He made only one public appearance—to accept his party's nomination for president. By contrast, Harrison made many public appearances, but all at his Indianapolis home. He ran what was called a front-porch campaign. From his home's front steps, he gave about one hundred speeches to thousands of visitors, including newspaper reporters from across the United States. These reporters then wrote about Harrison's speeches for readers in their home-towns. Other Republicans, including James Blaine, crossed the United States, speaking in support of Harrison.

This large ball was part of Harrison's front-porch campaign.
The ball had various slogans written on the panels.

CAMPAIGN HOAX

In one strange event during the Harrison campaign, Charles Murchison, a California Republican, wrote a letter to the British ambassador in Washington, Sir Lionel Sackville-West. In the letter, Murchison pretended to have been born in Great Britain and asked the ambassador for his advice on whether to vote for Cleveland or Harrison. Sackville-West wrote back that Cleveland was the better choice. Murchison sent Sackville-West's letter to the Republican Party. The party released the letter to the press in late October, just before the election. Republicans then claimed the British were interfering in the election. Not knowing that the ambassador had been tricked into writing the letter, newspapers around the country carried headlines demanding that President Cleveland send the ambassador back to Great Britain. This controversy helped the Republicans stir up opposition to Cleveland.

Grover Cleveland had championed many unpopular policies, which gave the Republicans plenty of ammunition in their campaign. For instance, Cleveland and the Democrats opposed tariffs. Republicans argued that Cleveland's no-tariff policy, which allowed many inexpensive products into the country from overseas, caused job loss and business closures in the United States. High tariffs, the Republicans said, would eliminate foreign competition and allow U.S. businesses to make more money. For this reason, many wealthy U.S. business owners supported the Republicans.

Cleveland had vetoed a popular veterans' pension bill. In a symbolic gesture of friendship with the South,

This campaign ribbon shows Benjamin Harrison (top) and his running mate, Levi Morton (bottom).

✧ ──────────────

he had offered to return old Confederate battle flags, captured during the Civil War, to Southern states. Republicans were outraged, claiming the president was not supporting the military and those who had fought for the Union in the Civil War. Republicans also pointed out that several members of Cleveland's Democratic Party had opposed the Civil War in the 1860s. They accused some Democrats of being Confederate sympathizers or, worse, traitors to the United States.

The Republicans praised Harrison's Civil War record and pointed out that Cleveland had not fought in the war. This campaign tactic of focusing on a candidate's military service was called waving the bloody shirt. In every presidential campaign since the end of the Civil War, the Republicans had promoted their party as the one that had won the war, and the Democrats as the party of the Confederacy. They reminded voters about Abraham Lincoln, the first Republican president, and the sacrifices made by Republicans to defeat the South. Such campaign messages made strong impressions on Northern voters, many of whom were Union war veterans or relatives of soldiers who had fought in the war. Finally, Republicans spoke about running a strong national government, which also set them apart from the Democrats, who favored the power of states over that of the central government.

Many veterans, such as those pictured here at the National Home for Disabled Volunteer Soldiers, lived with constant reminders of the sacrifices they had made during the Civil War.

HARRISON ELECTED

U.S. presidential elections operate through the Electoral College. According to this system, each state has a certain number of electoral votes based on that state's population. States such as New York and California, where many people live, have more electoral votes than states such as Maryland and Wyoming, where fewer people live. Whichever presidential candidate wins a majority of the state's popular votes (votes from citizens) wins all the state's electoral votes. Thus candidates often focus on winning the majority of popular votes in big states, so they can gather the most electoral votes.

The race between Harrison and Cleveland demonstrated the Electoral College in action. On Election Day, the popular vote was very close. Cleveland won about 5,534,000 votes to Harrison's 5,444,000. Cleveland carried every Southern state, as expected. But Harrison carried two important swing states—Indiana and New York. Winning New York was the key to Harrison's victory. With New York's many electoral votes, Harrison was able to tally 233 votes in the Electoral College. Cleveland had only 168 electoral votes. Therefore, Harrison won the election, even though he had fewer popular votes than Cleveland.

Boss Platt had played an important role in making sure New York went to the Republicans. He strongly disliked President Cleveland, who opposed political machines (party networks) like the one Platt controlled in New York. Many believed that Platt bribed hundreds of voters and public officials to make sure Harrison won in New York. Rumors circulated in Indiana that Harrison's supporters paid people to vote for him there too.

How a Bill Becomes Law

The federal government has three branches, or parts: the executive branch, made up of the president, the president's staff, and government agencies such as the State Department; the judicial branch, made up of the courts; and the legislative branch, made up of Congress. Congress consists of the House of Representatives and the Senate, with members from each state.

For a bill (proposed law) to become law, it must pass the House and Senate and then be signed by the president. If the president does not like a bill sent from Congress, the president can veto, or reject, it. When one political party controls the Congress and the presidency, it is easier to pass laws, since the president and the majority of the Senate and House are political allies (partners). This was the situation when Benjamin Harrison took office.

Regardless of the rumors, Benjamin Harrison had won the presidency. He had finally risen to the greatness and fame that his family had long expected of him. With his election, Harrison had equaled his grandfather's accomplishment. He also became the first president whose grandfather had been president as well.

The campaign proved to be very liberating for Benjamin Harrison. Instead of separating himself from his grandfather as he had earlier in his life, Harrison finally embraced his connection to the late president. Supporters passed out handbills (small posters) and souvenirs picturing Harrison and his

Benjamin Harrison's grandfather, William Henry Harrison (left), was president for a short time in 1841. One month into his term, he died of pneumonia.

✧ ————————————

grandfather together, reminding voters of the connection between the two famous generals.

In addition to winning the presidency, the Republicans also took control of the House of Representatives and strengthened their majority in the Senate that year. For the first time in several years, Republicans controlled the presidency and both houses of Congress. With all this success, the Republicans had high expectations for the new president when he arrived in Washington.

Adding to the excitement that year, Russell Harrison and his wife, Mary, had a baby girl, whom they named Marthena. Mary Harrison McKee and her husband, James, also had a baby girl, named Mary. The Harrisons then had three grandchildren. The whole family—including the Harrison children and grandchildren—looked forward to moving to Washington, D.C., where they would all live in the White House.

Benjamin Harrison was inaugurated on a cold, rainy day in 1889. The weather did not prevent thousands of spectators from attending the event.

CHAPTER SIX

A NEW PRESIDENT HARRISON

This sense of single and personal responsibility to the people has strongly held our Presidents to a good conscience, and to a high discharge of their duties.

—Benjamin Harrison

On March 4, 1889, Benjamin Harrison took the oath of office as the twenty-third president of the United States. Forty-eight years earlier, on the same date, his grandfather had been sworn in as the nation's ninth president.

Inauguration Day was cold and rainy. Harrison gave his inaugural address with an uncovered head in front of the U.S. Capitol. Speaking without a hat was unusual in 1889, but William Henry Harrison, in a show of braving the elements, had done the same in 1841—and Benjamin Harrison wanted to be inaugurated as his grandfather had been. While his grandfather's inaugural speech had been the longest in U.S. history, taking about two hours to complete, Benjamin Harrison's was much shorter, only about four thousand words and lasting well under an hour.

In his speech, Benjamin Harrison spoke about the country's needs, including tariff protection for businesses, new states in the West, and a strong foreign policy and armed forces. He also talked about the importance of equal rights for African Americans, who had been victims of discrimination and violence since winning their freedom in the Civil War.

After the speech, Harrison and his family traveled to the White House by horse-drawn carriage. Despite the bad weather, more than forty thousand people cheered them on. Harrison, his family, and Vice President Levi Morton then watched a four-hour parade of bands and business, community, and political groups pass in front of the White House.

—————————————— ✧ ——————————————

Bands paraded by the White House on Harrison's Inauguration Day.

That night, about twelve thousand people attended an inaugural ball, a party for the new president, held at the Federal Pension Office at Fifth and F Streets in Washington. The Marine Corps Band played music as couples danced and the First Family greeted guests. The menu included chicken soup, oysters, turtle, chicken salad, ham sandwiches, lobster salad, and turkey.

✧ ————————
Harrison's Inaugural Ball was held in the Federal Pension Office (inset, bottom left).

PRESIDENTIAL APPOINTMENTS

With Harrison's victory, Republicans were jubilant. They had recaptured the presidency. Many of Harrison's supporters, including Boss Platt, Matthew Quay, James Blaine, and Republican Party vice chair James Clarkson of Iowa, expected to receive the "spoils of victory" (gifts and favors) from the new president. Such spoils usually included top jobs in the new administration, jobs for family and friends, and building projects—such as dams and canals—that would bring business to their home states.

Some supporters had spent thousands of dollars seeing to it that Harrison got elected. John Wanamaker, a rich business owner from Philadelphia, had spent millions. Rumors spread that Matthew Quay, political boss of Pennsylvania, had even bribed people and faked voting records to make sure that Harrison won the election. He and all the other people who worked for Harrison's election expected to be paid for their hard work.

After the election, Matthew Quay went to the new president to discuss his reward for helping with a winning campaign. But Harrison surprised Quay. A deeply religious man, Harrison said that God had elected him president, not supporters like Quay. Quay was furious. He felt that all his hard work had been for nothing. Quay later told a reporter that Harrison did not understand how many Republicans "were compelled to approach the gates of the penitentiary [risk going to prison] to make him President."

Mostly, Harrison awarded jobs based on merit—on a job-seeker's skills, qualifications, and past achievements. For instance, Harrison appointed a promising young New York

Harrison appointed Frederick Douglass (left) as U.S. ambassador to Haiti.

◇ ─────────

politician, Theodore Roosevelt, as civil service commissioner. He appointed Frederick Douglass, a former slave and nationally known civil rights leader, as U.S. ambassador to Haiti. Awarding jobs based on merit alone was almost unheard of in late nineteenth-century U.S. politics.

Harrison did reward some supporters for their help with his election. John Wanamaker, for example, became the postmaster general, and James Blaine became secretary of

Harrison appointed John Wanamaker postmaster general as a reward for his help with the campaign.

state. Responding to pressure from political supporters, Harrison made James Clarkson the first assistant postmaster general.

FULFILLING CAMPAIGN PROMISES

With control of Congress and the White House, the Republicans started quickly on their program for the country. They focused on their biggest campaign promise of 1888—creating high tariffs. The Republicans' big-business allies wanted the tariffs passed quickly, so their companies would make more money as soon as possible. Most congressional Democrats opposed the higher tariffs, but they did not have enough votes in Congress to stop Republicans from passing a new tariff law.

With Harrison's support, Congress passed the McKinley Tariff Act. This law, named after U.S. representative William McKinley of Ohio, raised tariffs by as much as 48 percent on many imported goods. Democrats criticized the new tariffs, saying they were too high. They warned that high tariffs would lead to high prices for U.S. goods. Indeed, within a year of the tariff bill's passage, prices for many products did increase.

CIVIL RIGHTS PIONEER

Protecting the rights of African Americans was another top priority for Harrison. Enslaved black Americans had won their freedom with the Civil War, and black men had won the right to vote in 1870. But despite these changes, blacks were routinely discriminated against, especially in the South. Some white people often threatened black men with violence to keep them from voting.

To protect the voting rights of black Southerners, Harrison wanted the federal government—instead of Southern officeholders—to supervise voter registration and elections in the South. In late 1889, Congressman Henry Cabot Lodge and Senators George Hoar and William Chandler, all Republicans, drafted a bill that reflected the president's ideas. Harrison pushed hard for the bill's passage.

Almost all Democrats opposed the bill. They believed that if the federal government supervised Southern elections, the Democratic Party's dominance in the South might end. They knew that black people overwhelmingly supported the Republican Party, the party of Abraham Lincoln, who had freed the slaves during the Civil War. Thus Democrats did not want to make it easier for African Americans to vote.

Democrats nicknamed the bill the Force Bill, saying it allowed the federal government to send the army to the South to supervise elections by force. This claim was untrue, but the nickname influenced many members of Congress to oppose the bill. In addition, the political bosses President Harrison had angered earlier came back to hurt him. Matthew Quay, Harrison's former campaign manager and then a leading Republican senator, wanted revenge for what he considered the president's poor treatment of him. He fought against the bill in the Senate, partly because he knew how much Harrison wanted it to pass. Although the bill passed the House of Representatives in a close vote—155 to 149—it did not pass the Senate.

SHERMAN SILVER PURCHASE ACT

During Harrison's first two years in office, six new states joined the Union—the most states admitted during any presidential administration. These states were all in the West. North and South Dakota, Montana, and Washington joined in 1889. Idaho and Wyoming joined in 1890. Harrison supported the westward expansion of the United States, just as he had during his time as a U.S. senator.

The new states were strongly Republican. Their voters sent mostly Republicans to serve in the House of Representatives, and the states' Republican-controlled legislatures elected Republicans to the U.S. Senate. These new western Congress members helped strengthen Republican

The economy of many cities in the western United States, including Virginia City, Nevada (above), centered on silver.

control of Congress. But the westerners also had specific concerns that they expected President Harrison to address.

Most of the country's silver mines were in western states. Representatives and senators from the new western states and from Nevada and Colorado supported the interests of the large silver mines in their states. This "silver bloc" of sixteen western Congress members was very powerful. In exchange for support of the McKinley Tariff Act, the silver bloc wanted the federal government to purchase silver produced in western states.

Pressured by the silver bloc, Congress passed the Sherman Silver Purchase Act of 1890. This law required the federal government to buy 4.5 million ounces of silver each month— almost the entire monthly production of silver in the United States. Much of the silver would be made into coins.

The U.S. Treasury paid for the silver with certificates that could be traded in at any time for either gold or silver. At first, silver prices rose, which made the silver companies happy. People holding the silver certificates were also pleased—their certificates were worth a lot of money. However, by late 1890, silver prices had dropped as the supply of silver increased. So people began asking for payment for their certificates in gold, which was worth more than silver.

With more and more people receiving gold for their certificates, the government began running out of gold. Soon, the loss of so much gold caused a rapid drop in the value of paper money, damaging the U.S. economy. Many businesses closed, and some people lost their jobs. It soon became clear that the Sherman Silver Purchase Act had been a bad idea.

◇ ————————————

This political cartoon treats the Sherman Silver Purchase Act symbolically. A woman representing the U.S. economy drowns in a sea of silver, while Uncle Sam tries to save her.

Harrison supported the growth of the U.S. Navy during his term as president. This steel ship was named after his home state, Indiana.

FOREIGN POLICY

In his inaugural address, Harrison had talked about a strong role for the United States in the world. In the early 1880s, President Chester Arthur had begun the construction of the "steel navy." His plan was to replace the navy's old wooden and mostly wind-powered ships with new steel ships driven by powerful steam engines. Harrison agreed with this program and wanted to continue it. He asked Congress for money to construct several new warships, including large battleships. Although Congress did not permit the building of as many ships as the president wanted, it authorized the creation of seven new steel warships during Harrison's administration.

Trust and Antitrust

With the beginning of the Industrial Age, large businesses thrived throughout the United States. These businesses, such as steel and iron manufacturers, had a lot of money and power. Steel and iron were used to manufacture trains, railroad tracks, ships, and other items that were important to U.S. business, transportation, defense, communications, and finance.

Large businesses in the same industry, such as the steel industry, often worked together, forming associations called trusts. A trust would buy up the competition and set high prices for its products. Since the businesses in the trust were all working together, with no competition, buyers had no choice but to pay the high prices.

Many people worried that trusts were cheating consumers and hurting the U.S. economy. Some states, especially those in the South and West, passed laws to regulate trusts and decrease their power. But such laws had little effect. Businesses would simply move out of states with "trust-busting" laws to states with friendlier laws for business, such as Delaware and New Jersey. Many Americans felt that the only way to fight trusts was for Congress to act against them.

In the first year of Harrison's term, Senator John Sherman of Ohio introduced the Sherman Antitrust Act for a vote in the U.S. Senate. This bill restricted trusts and gave the federal government the power to sue them. Many members of Congress voted for the law because they believed it was good politics—that is, the public supported antitrust laws, and Congress members wanted to please voters.

But the language of the Sherman bill was unclear. That meant the law would be hard to enforce. Big businesses generally did not oppose the law for this reason—the law was

Senator John Sherman

——————— ✧ ———————

so unclear that business owners thought the government would be unable to use it to stop their questionable activities. The Sherman Antitrust Act quickly passed the Senate by a vote of 52 to 1. On June 20, 1890, the House of Representatives also passed the act, without any "no" votes.

Although he supported the Sherman Antitrust Act, President Harrison did little to use it. He did not consider regulating big business to be very important. Additionally, most of the large companies affected by the Sherman Antitrust Act were big supporters of Harrison and the Republican Party. Harrison and his advisers knew it would be bad politics to fight their big businesses supporters. Thus Harrison's government brought very few antitrust cases against these businesses.

Harrison was not afraid to use the stronger navy in disputes with other countries. For instance, in 1890 a disagreement developed among the United States, Canada, and Great Britain over seal hunting in the Bering Sea, next to Alaska. Seals were highly prized for their fur, skin, and oil, and all three countries had significant sealing industries. Harrison believed that only the United States should be allowed to hunt seals in the Bering Sea, and he was willing to use the navy to keep other nations from hunting there. Eventually, all countries involved agreed to discuss their differences and avoided fighting each other.

Harrison and Secretary of State James Blaine also wanted to expand U.S. power in Latin America (the mostly Spanish-speaking nations south of the United States). Harrison and Blaine sought to increase trade with the countries there and to reduce the influence of Great Britain, which had long-standing ties to many Latin American nations. From October 1889 to April 1890, leaders of many Latin American countries came to Washington to meet with U.S. officials at the Pan-American Conference, the first such meeting of these nations. The conference led to trade agreements between the United States and several Latin American countries, such as Brazil, El Salvador, Honduras, and Guatemala.

TRAGEDY OUT WEST

Although Harrison fought for the rights of African Americans, he showed little support for Native Americans, the original inhabitants of North America. Harrison backed the westward expansion of the United States, including taking Native American lands to make room for white settlers.

In late 1890, Harrison sent thousands of U.S. soldiers to South Dakota, where the Lakota Sioux were trying to hang onto their remaining lands. On December 29, a group of soldiers clashed with a band of Lakota men, women, and children at South Dakota's Wounded Knee Creek. During this encounter, the U.S. troops killed several hundred Native Americans. Twenty-five soldiers also died.

Although Harrison ordered an investigation into the army's conduct during the battle, he did not oppose the soldiers' actions. The government's investigation, reflecting that era's prejudice against Native Americans, blamed the Lakota for the encounter more than it blamed the soldiers. The massacre at Wounded Knee was the last major clash

———————————— ✧ ————————————

U.S. soldiers fire on the Lakota at Wounded Knee Creek in 1890.

First Lady Carrie Harrison

During her husband's presidency, Carrie Harrison was an active First Lady. In 1889 she installed the White House's first Christmas tree, in part to please her three grandchildren. She became the first president of the Daughters of the American Revolution, a patriotic organization. Carrie Harrison also began the White House china collection (still displayed in the White House's China Room), and she had electric lights—a brand-new invention—installed in the White House.

◇ ─────────────
This portrait of Carrie Harrison was taken on July 9, 1889.

between U.S. soldiers and Native Americans. Afterward, the U.S. government took most of the remaining lands owned by Native Americans and gave them to white settlers. Most surviving Native Americans were forced onto government-run reservations, where they lived in poverty, without the rights or freedoms of other Americans.

LIFE IN THE WHITE HOUSE

President Harrison had plenty of government work to keep him busy, but he always made time for his family. With Harrison's two grown children and their spouses and children living there, the White House was truly a family home. What's more, Carrie's father, sister, and niece lived there too.

The family liked their privacy and tried to have as few guests as possible. But presidents often need to entertain visiting foreign leaders, members of Congress, and other politicians. When the Harrisons occasionally did have a

———————————— ✧ ————————————

Harrison's three grandchildren and his adult son, Russell, pose on the lawn of the White House with two of the family's pets.

party, they did not serve alcohol. Their religious beliefs did not allow it.

Harrison often stopped working at noon to spend time with his three grandchildren, Benjamin, Mary, and Marthena. The children were permitted to keep pets in the White House. One was a goat named Old Whiskers. One day the goat escaped from the White House. President Harrison chased it down the street, waving his cane and followed by his grandchildren.

CHAPTER SEVEN

HOME STRETCH

I am very happy here in
Indianapolis. . . . Home is a pretty good place.
—Benjamin Harrison

In 1890 elections for the House of Representatives were held across the nation. By then, many voters had become dissatisfied with President Harrison and the Republican Congress. Prices had increased, and many voters blamed the Republican Party and its passage of high tariffs. The Sherman Silver Purchase Act had also hurt the U.S. economy. What's more, the Congress of 1889–1890 had spent approximately one billion dollars in one year, becoming the first "Billion-Dollar Congress" in U.S. history. When Harrison had taken office in 1888, the government had had a large supply of money. By 1890 that money had disappeared, replaced by a deficit (more debt than cash) of many millions of dollars. Most voters thought the government was spending too much.

On Election Day, the voters took their anger out on Benjamin Harrison and his congressional allies. About eighty Republicans in Congress lost their reelection bids and were replaced by Democrats. The Democratic Party took control of the House of Representatives, which meant that President Harrison would face more congressional opposition to his proposals.

HOME AND ABROAD

As the United States continued its westward expansion, President Harrison wanted to make sure that the government preserved unspoiled western lands for future generations to enjoy. He personally loved the western landscape, although he had seen it only in paintings and photographs.

Harrison enjoyed images of western landscapes, such as this painting of Wyoming by Thomas Moran.

In 1891 Congress, with the president's support, passed the Forest Reserve Act. It permitted the government to create national forest and wilderness preserves. Within a month of the law's passage, Harrison had created a forest reserve in Wyoming, next to Yellowstone National Park. In all, President Harrison established twenty-two million acres of national forests throughout the western United States during his term in office.

In the foreign policy arena, the United States came very close to war with the South American nation of Chile. Disagreements between the two countries dated to the 1880s, when the United States had supported Peru and Bolivia in a war against Chile. In addition, the United States had sided with the Chilean government during an 1890 civil war, which the government lost. The government that emerged after the civil war was angry at the United States for supporting the former regime.

Further inflaming the situation, in October 1891, two U.S. sailors were killed in a fight with Chileans in the port city of Valparaiso, Chile, where their warship had docked. Many Americans were furious. President Harrison sent more ships to Chile, and on January 25, 1892, he asked Congress for a declaration of war against the South American nation. Without the strength to resist the U.S. Navy, the Chilean government apologized and paid the United States seventy-five thousand dollars as compensation for the sailors' deaths.

A DIFFICULT YEAR

The year 1892 was difficult for the United States as well as President Harrison. Many Americans were fed up with the president's support for big business. Laborers began to organize unions to fight for higher wages and better working conditions.

In Homestead, Pennsylvania, at a steel plant owned by Andrew Carnegie (a powerful Republican supporter), the workers went on strike. They refused to work until the company agreed to pay them fair wages. In response, the company brought in nonunion replacement workers and hired security guards to protect the replacements. In July 1892, several union members were killed in a gunfight with security guards. The incident stirred up resentment against President Harrison and the Republicans. Many Americans believed that the president cared more about wealthy business owners such as Andrew Carnegie than he did for ordinary working people.

✧ ————————
Union members clashed with armed guards during a famous strike in Homestead, Pennsylvania, in 1892.

HAWAIIAN ISLANDS

Late in his term, President Harrison attempted to annex, or take control of, the Hawaiian Islands—located southwest of the mainland United States in the Pacific Ocean. Hawaii then was an independent country. With the help of U.S. soldiers, John Stevens (U.S. ambassador to Hawaii) and wealthy American planter Sanford Dole overthrew Hawaiian queen

Liliuokalani in January 1893. Dole took over the Hawaiian government, and Stevens declared Hawaii to be part of the United States. But Congress did not want to reward outgoing president Harrison by bringing Hawaii into the United States before Harrison left office in March. So it took no action. It left the decision of what to do about Hawaii to the next president.

Hawaii's Queen Liliuokalani

As the 1892 election approached, Benjamin Harrison was uncertain whether he should run for president again. He still had many enemies among the political bosses. Men like Thomas Platt, Matthew Quay, and James Clarkson had never forgiven the president for not rewarding them and their supporters. They wanted to prevent Harrison from being nominated again. Other opponents criticized Harrison for his policies such as high tariffs and the Sherman Silver Purchase Act. Ordinary Americans were angry at Harrison for siding with big business instead of striking workers.

Harrison was tired of working in Washington and tired of being criticized by his opponents and the public. What's more, his wife, Carrie, had become ill. Early in 1892, she had contracted tuberculosis, a serious lung disease. But the government kept her illness secret from the public. Despite this and other problems, most political leaders still considered Harrison the best choice as the Republican nominee for president.

A HALF-HEARTED CAMPAIGN

James Blaine, who had resigned as secretary of state, was also a presidential candidate in 1892. Harrison and he were rivals, and his candidacy angered the president. So Harrison decided to run for reelection, in part to keep the nomination away from Blaine. William McKinley had announced his candidacy as well.

At the Republican National Convention, Blaine and McKinley received substantial support, but not enough for the nomination. In fact, President Harrison was renominated on the first ballot. On the Democratic side, former president Grover Cleveland was again nominated for president.

Thus the election of 1892 would feature the same candidates as the election of four years earlier.

Neither candidate campaigned very much during the race. By fall Carrie Harrison was seriously ill. Benjamin did not want to leave her side and gave none of the front-porch speeches for which he had become famous in 1888. Out of respect for Carrie Harrison, Cleveland also made very few public appearances.

✧ ————————
Harrison's portrait appeared on the cover of Harper's Weekly *after he was announced as the Republican candidate for the presidential election of 1892.*

A new political party, the Populist Party, ran a candidate for president for the first time in 1892. The Populists were seen as the party of the common people. They supported workers over big business and also supported low tariffs. The Populist candidate, James Weaver, attracted the support of many farmers and laborers in the Midwest and West. These farmers were angry at Harrison's policies, especially high tariffs.

Carrie Harrison died on October 25, two weeks before Election Day. Her death greatly saddened the president. He lost all interest in the campaign and his reelection. On

✧ ————————————

People paid their last respects to Carrie Harrison in the East Room of the White House. She died in 1892.

November 8, Grover Cleveland won a big victory, with nearly 400,000 more popular votes and 132 more electoral votes than Harrison. James Weaver did surprisingly well, winning more than 1 million votes and Electoral College victories in four states.

Although Harrison had been defeated, he was not unhappy. He told family members that he felt he had been freed from the prison of the presidency, with its many responsibilities. He looked forward to going home to Indiana.

BACK TO INDIANA

Upon leaving office, Benjamin Harrison and his family returned to Indianapolis, to the three-story brick house he and Carrie had shared for so many years. Harrison resumed his law practice. Although still grieving over Carrie's death, he began a very active life as an ex-president. His law practice grew, as many people wanted to hire a former president as their lawyer.

The government of Venezuela, involved in a border dispute with the neighboring country of British Guiana (modern-day Guyana), hired Harrison to represent Venezuela in an international court in Paris, France. Harrison worked hard on the case. He filed an eight-hundred-page brief, or legal paper, with the court and argued the case in court for more than twenty-five hours. Eventually, the court sided with British Guiana, but Harrison's legal arguments impressed many people around the world. His law practice grew even more because of this case.

Harrison also wrote articles about the presidency and important issues of the time for national magazines. In

Mary Scott Lord Dimmick was Harrison's second wife.

✧ ————————————————

1894 he moved briefly to California, where he taught a class on constitutional law at Stanford University south of San Francisco.

In 1896, four years after his wife's death, Benjamin Harrison remarried. At the age of sixty-two, he wed Mary Scott Lord Dimmick, age thirty-seven. Mary was Carrie Harrison's niece. For many years, she had lived in the White House and assisted Carrie with social events. When Carrie grew sick, Mary helped care for her.

Harrison's grown children were upset about the marriage and the age difference between their father and their cousin Mary. They were so unhappy that they refused to come to the wedding ceremony. One year later, the couple had a daughter, whom they named Elizabeth Harrison.

Many Republicans wanted Harrison to run for president again in 1896. But Harrison declined and supported party nominee William McKinley in the election, which McKinley won. In gratitude for Harrison's support, President McKinley appointed Harrison to the Permanent Court of Arbitration, an international court used to settle disagreements between countries. Harrison also traveled widely throughout the United States for both business and pleasure. He made a short trip to Europe, his first.

In early 1901, Harrison caught the flu. The illness worsened and became pneumonia. Harrison grew sicker and never recovered. On March 13, 1901, the former president died in Indianapolis. He was buried next to his first wife, Carrie, at Crown Hill Cemetery in Indianapolis.

✧ ————————————

Benjamin Harrison's grave is in Crown Hill Cemetery in Indianapolis, Indiana.

SITES TO VISIT

Modern visitors can learn more about Benjamin Harrison at several sites around the nation. Benjamin Harrison's house in Indianapolis is open to visitors. The home contains many mementos from Harrison's life and some of the original furniture from when he lived there.

Visitors at the Benjamin Harrison house in Indianapolis can see some of Harrison's personal possessions, such as his top hat and its carrying case.

HARRISON'S LEGACY

For many years after his death, Benjamin Harrison was not highly regarded as a president. Many critics thought his policies, such as high tariffs and silver purchases, caused high prices and harmed the country's economy. However, in the more than one hundred years since his death, many people have come to think more favorably of Benjamin Harrison, especially in the area of international relations.

Harrison's strong foreign policy and his support for a powerful navy helped set the stage for the United States to eventually become a world power.

Harrison's attitudes about race relations and his concern for the civil rights of African Americans were unusual for his era. His attempt to pass a federal voting rights act in the 1880s was also ahead of its time. It took about eighty more years, until 1965, for Congress to pass a federal law protecting minority citizens' voting rights.

Although Benjamin Harrison struggled with family expectations and his grandfather's legacy for most of his life, in the end, the grandson of a president enjoyed a full career. Many of his presidential accomplishments helped bring the United States into the twentieth century as a powerful, wealthy nation.

Timeline

1833   Benjamin Harrison is born on August 20 in North Bend, Ohio.

1838   Benjamin starts school in a one-room schoolhouse on his father's farm.

1841   William Henry Harrison, Benjamin's grandfather, becomes the ninth president of the United States. He dies only one month after his inauguration.

1847   Benjamin and his brother Archibald move to Cincinnati to attend Farmers College.

1850   Benjamin graduates from Farmers College. Benjamin's mother, Elizabeth Harrison, dies after giving birth. Benjamin enrolls at Miami University in Oxford, Ohio.

1852   Harrison graduates with honors from Miami University.

1853   Harrison marries Caroline Scott in Oxford, Ohio. Harrison's father, John Harrison, is elected to the U.S. Congress.

1854   Harrison becomes a practicing attorney. The Harrisons' first child, Russell Benjamin Harrison, is born in Oxford, Ohio.

1856   Harrison joins the newly formed Republican Party.

1857   Harrison is elected Indianapolis city attorney.

1858   The Harrisons' second child, Mary Scott Harrison, is born. Harrison becomes the Indiana Republican Party secretary.

1860   Harrison wins his first statewide election, becoming the Indiana supreme court reporter.

1861   Southern troops fire on Fort Sumter in Charleston, South Carolina, beginning the Civil War.

1862 Harrison enters military service as a second lieutenant with the Seventieth Indiana Volunteer Regiment. He is soon promoted to the rank of colonel.

1864 Harrison and his regiment fight against Confederate troops during the Battle of Atlanta and the Battle of Nashville. Harrison is reelected as Indiana supreme court reporter.

1865 The Civil War ends. Harrison is promoted to brigadier general and retires from military service.

1866 Harrison acts as the U.S. government's attorney in the case of *Ex parte Milligan*.

1868 Harrison turns down offers to run for the U.S. House of Representatives and for Indiana governor.

1872 Harrison tries to run for Indiana governor but loses the Republican Party nomination to Thomas Browne.

1876 Harrison runs for governor of Indiana but loses the election.

1879 President Rutherford B. Hayes appoints Harrison to the Mississippi River Commission.

1880 Harrison leads the Indiana delegation to the Republican National Convention.

1881 Harrison is elected a U.S. senator from Indiana.

1882 Congress passes the Chinese Exclusion Act, a law that Harrison opposes.

1887 Harrison loses his bid for reelection to U.S. Senate.

1888 Harrison defeats Grover Cleveland to win the presidential election.

1889 Harrison is inaugurated as the twenty-third president of the United States.

1890 Congress passes the Dependent and Disability Pensions Act, the Sherman Antitrust Act, the McKinley Tariff, and the Sherman Silver Purchase Act. U.S. troops massacre a group of Lakota Sioux at Wounded Knee Creek in South Dakota.

1891 Congress passes the Forest Reserve Act, which gives presidents the power to create national forests.

1892 Workers at the Homestead mill in Pennsylvania go on strike. Harrison's wife Caroline dies of tuberculosis. Harrison loses reelection as president.

1893 Harrison returns to Indianapolis and resumes his law practice.

1894 Harrison moves to California to teach a law class at Stanford University.

1896 Harrison marries Mary Scott Lord Dimmick.

1897 Harrison's third child, Elizabeth Harrison, is born.

1901 Harrison dies on March 13 at the age of sixty-seven.

SOURCE NOTES

7 Harry J. Sievers, *Benjamin Harrison: Hoosier Warrior* (Newtown, CT: American Political Biography Press, 1996), 8.

10 William A. Degregorio, *The Complete Book of U.S. Presidents* (Fort Lee, NJ: Barricade Books, 2001), 333.

17 Ibid.

21 Ibid., 341.

31 Benjamin Harrison to Caroline Harrison, May 13, 1864. Benjamin Harrison Papers, Library of Congress.

34 Paul F. Boller Jr., *Presidential Anecdotes* (New York: Oxford University Press, 1981), 183.

34 Degregorio, *The Complete Book of U.S. Presidents*, 334.

36 Benjamin Harrison to Caroline Harrison, September 2, 1864. Benjamin Harrison Papers, Library of Congress.

37 James M. Perry, *Touched with Fire: Five Presidents and the Civil War Battles That Made Them* (New York: Public Affairs, 2003), 252.

38 Sievers, *Benjamin Harrison*, 264.

41 Perry, *Touched with Fire*, 259.

41 Ibid.

43 Sievers, *Benjamin Harrison*, 316.

57 Degregorio, *The Complete Book of U.S. Presidents*, 341.

59 Leonard Levy and Louis Fisher, eds., *Encyclopedia of the American Presidency* (New York: Simon & Schuster, 1994), 729.

73 Degregorio, *The Complete Book of U.S. Presidents*, 341.

76 James A. Kiehl, "The Unmaking of a President: 1889–92," *Pennsylvania History* 39, 4:469.

91 Boller, *Presidential Anecdotes*, 184.

SELECTED BIBLIOGRAPHY

American Heritage. *American Heritage Book of the Presidents and Famous Americans.* Vol. 7. New York: Dell Publishing, 1967.

"Benjamin Harrison (1889–1893)." *American President.org* http://www.americanpresident.org/history/benjaminharrison

Boller, Paul F., Jr. *Presidential Campaigns.* New York: Oxford University Press, 1984.

Degregorio, William A. *The Complete Book of U.S. Presidents.* Fort Lee, NJ: Barricade Books, 2001.

Geib, George. *Benjamin Harrison.* Indianapolis: Indiana Historical Society, 2000.

Heidler, David S., and Jeanne T. Heidler. *Encyclopedia of the American Civil War: A Political, Social, and Military History.* Santa Barbara, CA: ABC-Clio, Inc., 1994.

Kane, Joseph, Steven Anzovin, and Jane Podell, eds. *Facts about the Presidents.* New York: H. W. Wilson and Co., 2001.

Perry, James M. *Touched with Fire: Five Presidents and the Civil War Battles That Made Them.* New York: Public Affairs, 2003.

Sievers, Harry J. *Benjamin Harrison: Hoosier Warrior.* Newtown, CT: American Political Biography Press, 1996.

Socolofsky, Homer E., and Allan B. Spetter. *The Presidency of Benjamin Harrison.* Lawrence: University Press of Kansas, 1987.

FURTHER READING AND WEBSITES

American President.Org
http://www.americanpresident.org
This site includes in-depth information on each U.S. president. Visitors can learn about Benjamin Harrison's life and presidency, as well as the lives and work of every other U.S. president.

Arnold, James R. *The Civil War*. Minneapolis: Lerner Publications Company, 2005.

Edge, Laura. *Andrew Carnegie*. Minneapolis: Lerner Publications Company, 2004.

Greene, Meg. *Into the Land of Freedom: African Americans in Reconstruction*. Minneapolis: Lerner Publications Company, 2004.

Indiana's Storyteller: Connecting People to the Past
http://www.indianahistory.org
This site features information on Indiana history and the life of Benjamin Harrison.

Landau, Elaine. *Fleeing to Freedom on the Underground Railraod: The Courageous Slaves, Agents, and Conductors*. Minneapolis: Twenty-First Century Books, 2006.

Lester, Julius. *To Be a Slave*. New York: Dial Books, 1999.

Levine, Ellen. *If You Traveled the Underground Railroad*. New York: Scholastic Press, 1993.

Roberts, Jeremy. *Abraham Lincoln*. Minneapolis: Twenty-First Century Books, 2004.

Streissguth, Thomas. *Wounded Knee 1890: The End of the Plains Indian Wars*. New York: Facts on File, 1999.

Twain, Mark. *The Gilded Age: A Tale of Today*. 1873. Reprint, New York: Penguin Books, 2001.

Young, Jeff C. *Benjamin Harrison*. Berkeley Heights, NJ: Enslow Publishers, 2002.

INDEX

ABOUT THE AUTHOR

Bruce Adelson is the author of fourteen books for children and adults, including both sports and history titles. He has been a commentator for CBS Radio's *Major League Baseball Game of the Week* and the editor of *The Four Sport Stadium Guide*. His work has also been published in various newspapers and periodicals. Adelson is a lawyer and a former elementary school substitute teacher in Arlington, Virginia. He lives in Maryland with his wife and son.

✧

PHOTO ACKNOWLEDGMENTS

Images in this book are used with permission of: The White House, pp. 1, 7, 10, 21, 31, 43, 57, 73, 91; President Benjamin Harrison Home Indianapolis, pp. 2, 6, 11, 12, 14, 20, 33, 46, 56, 65, 67, 102; © Brown Brothers, pp. 15, 17, 30, 95; Library of Congress, pp. 22 (LC-USZ62-3775), 23 (LC-USZ62-23934), 27 (LC-USZ62-107503), 28 (LC-USZ62-58751), 36 (LC-USZ62-72803), 37 (LC-USZ62-102052), 38 (LC-DIG-cwpb-03405), 40 (LC-B8184-4541), 42 (LC-USZ62-5687), 44 (HABS, IND,49-IND, 10-2), 45 (LC-USZ62-13018), 47 (LC-DIG-cwpbh-04308), 49 (LC-DIG-cwpbh-03606), 58 (LC-USZ62-88699), 60 (LC-USZ62-89792), 62 (LC-USZ62-10176), 63 (LC-DIG-cwpbh-03700), 64 (LC-BH832-1329), 71 (LC-USZC4-12216), 72 (LC-USZ62-63418), 75 (LC-USZ62-60975), 77 (LC-DIG-cwpbh-05089), 78 (LC-USZ62-44258), 81 (LC-USZ62-107521), 82 (LC-USZ62-93406), 85 (LC-USZ62-67704), 87 (LC-USZ62-89867), 88 (LC-USZ62-25798), 89 (LC-USZ62-118058), 92 (LC-USZ62-37303), 94 (LC-USZ62-126046), 100 (LC-DIG-ggbain-04830), 101 (LC-USZ62-115422); © North Wind Picture Archives, pp. 50, 53, 61, 68, 74, 83, 97, 98; © California Historical Society, FN-25345, p. 54.

Cover: Library of Congress, (LC-USZ62-134885).